World Of Bells No. 3

Dorothy Malone Anthony

Merry Christmas
To Florence
From Russ

WH books

WALLACE-HOMESTEAD BOOK CO
1912 GRAND
DES MOINES, IOWA 50305

Library of Congress Catalog No. 76-0824
ISBN 0-87069-183-X

ITEM ON FRONT COVER

Cameo glass bell by DeVez. Glass is frosted background with two acid cuttings. Ormolu gold-washed handle with original chain and tassle-like gold metal clapper.

The technique for making cameo glass is the fusing of a clear and a colored layer of glass, then cutting away the top layer to leave desired design. Although this process was recorded in the first century Roman world, it had very little usage until the French started producing cameo glass during the 1800's. Artists in Paris and Nancy factories reached the crest of production at the very last of the century. DeVez was the signature of Monsieur de Varreux, art director of a glass works in Paris.

There is only one other such cameo glass bell known. It can be found in the Milan, Italy Historical Museum.

France, 1890, 9 1/4" high, 7 1/8" diameter.

Photography by Ren-Nett Studio, Fort Scott, Kansas.

Published in the United States of America By
Wallace-Homestead Book Co.
Box B1
Des Moines, Iowa 50304

CONTENTS

FOREWORD

With a goal of expanded bell knowledge, this book is presented as a continuation of WORLD OF BELLS, Books I and II. Again, the views presented are those of the author as a result of extensive research, many of the materials covered being of a controversial nature. This led to a choice in reaching logical conclusions.

So that classifications might be as representative as possible, several bells were borrowed from other collectors. The balance are the property of the author.

The writer gratefully acknowledges assistance in research from Mrs. Pratt Irby. Appreciation goes to Mr. Claud Brock and Mr. Gerald Ballantyne for their generous loan of unusual items.

UNIQUE BELL TRADITIONS

Tintinnabulatists who are enthusiastic enough to make use of this third of a series are familiar with the many ways bells have contributed to ageless cultures. There are a few customs not commonly known that merit observation.

Upon the death of a Spartan king, women walked the streets ringing bells to signal all households to put on signs of mourning.

An ancient Grecian custom of hanging a bell around the neck of a criminal on his way to execution led to a later variation by the Romans. They hung the bell around the neck of their Emperor to remind him that even at the pinnacle of his glory, he should shed prideful ways and recall the misery of his fellow man.

The "oven bell" rang in Feudal times to let tenants know that the oven of the lord of the manor was hot and ready to bake their bread.

The "pancake bell" rang on Shrove Tuesday to signify confession before Lent.

"Harvest and seeding" bells called laborers to work.

Many centuries ago the bell was used as a title deed to property in Scotland and was passed down through generations to show their right to the land.

Whistles, Rattles, and Whirligigs

TOP ROW—
1. Coral-and-whistle rattle of great popularity during 18th and 19th centuries. Invented by English silver and goldsmiths for children of royalty and wealthy families. The fad was carried to America during Colonial times when Martha Washington was known to have purchased one for a christening gift. They were passed down through generations. The coral teether was an amulet to protect against evil spirits. English hallmark, circa 1865. 5" long.

MIDDLE ROW—
1. Wheel toy made by Lehman Company in Germany. One of their Futurus brands that entertains by ringing of bell as it rolled across floor. Early 1900's.
2. Handle is nursery rhyme character, "Mary, Mary Quite Contrary," shown with basket over arm as she smells flower picked from nearby bush. Cast brass. 4½" high.
3. "Peter Rabbit," children's fairy tale favorite, as he nibbles lettuce leaf from the patch. On a familiar old English-style bell base that has seen some remodelling in an attempt to turn up the lower edge. Made in two parts but each of old brass that match and of an early period. 3¾" high.

BOTTOM ROW—
1. Old whistle-rattle from Jerry Smith toy collection, a two million dollar group being sold by Hall's (of Hallmark, Inc.), Kansas City. The wooden handle is a whistle for entertaining the child. He can shake the rattle of eight small bells with blue bead clappers. These stemmed from the superstition that blue beads could keep witches from robbing the cradle. The parasol-shaped wire rattles were popular among common people not able to afford silver novelties. Mid-19th century. American, 9" high.
2. Rag doll bell from Bobbs-Merrill, Inc. The popular toys originated with John Gruell in 1915 following which the story was published by Bobbs-Merrill. Modern. American, 6" high.

Whistles, Rattles, and Whirligigs

TOP ROW—
1. Three temple bells decorate a silvery whistle rattle that is more of a conversation piece than for practical purpose. To be worn around neck of adult as he entertains baby. Silver alloy. India.
2. Dumbbell-shaped rattle showing excessive usage. Has mark of Saart Bothers Company, makers of silver novelties in Attleboro, Massachusetts 1906-1937. Marked Sterling Silver. 3¼" long.
3. Rattle with ferris wheel-type of action. Simplicity of lines such as the ones on the handle went along with the austere colonial life. This makes it plausible for the mark "CC" to stand for Charles Candell, a 1795 New York City silversmith who signed his items in that manner. 6" long.

MIDDLE ROW—
1. Mexican crotal rattle in unusual shape. Has plastic teether ring handle. Bell is marked "Necho En Mexico, D. F. — Sterling."
2. A rattle with slit in bottom meant to hang from a ribbon. Of the crotal or sleighbell type. The word crotal stems from the Greek work, KROTALON, meaning rattle. Marked EPNS which stand for Electroplated Nickel Silver. This process was started by Elkington in England during 1840's then taken up by Rogers and Son here in America.
3. Traditional baby rattle on mother-of-pearl type teether ring. Closed end makes it of later vintage than those which are open. Mark of Webster Company, North Attleboro, Massachusetts since 1869. This company has sold its trademark and is now Webster Division of Reed and Barton but it still specializes in baby goods. Sterling.
4. Modern rattle by Towle, a silver manufacturing company in Newburyport, Massachusetts since 1882. Plastic teething ring handle. Whimsical face with red nose on rattle. Sterling.

BOTTOM ROW—
1. Miniature plastic rattle with painted design. Such celluloid toys were at peak of popularity in 1920's. American. 2¼" long.
2. Elephant rattle with mother-of-pearl stub teether handle. Small crotal adds to noise when shaken. Quite popular before and after turn of century. Has mark of Webster Company, North Attleboro, Massachusetts since 1869, specialists in silver baby goods. Circa 1900. Sterling.
3. Santa Claus rattle with mother-of-pearl teether handle. Has bag of toys on back not seen in photo. Shows enough usage dents to stir sentiments of the Indiana family who passed it down through generations for a span of eighty years. Late 1800's. Marked "Sterling-62D100."

Figural Porcelains

If there are no marks inside porcelain bells of this century, one clue to identification lies in the attachment of the clapper. The Japanese usually punch two holes in the top at back of bell body, then run a wire through these to hold the clapper. Those of Italian manufacture are fastened to a built-in ceramic bridge inside top of the bell.

TOP ROW—
1. and 2. Seem to be a matched pair of full figural bells. Made in Japan but workmanship is of good quality. 4¾" high.

MIDDLE ROW—
1. Oriental girl with good detail. Marked "Made in Occupied Japan" which indicates it was exported to the United States 1945-1952. Items with such labels are eagerly sought by collectors and becoming rather scarce. Occupied Japan articles were of varied workmanship according to who did the handpainting. All ages, from children to adult fine artists, participated. 4½" high.
2. Traditional bride and groom with very fine detail. One of the better Lefton China products imported from Japan, probably late 1950's. 2¾" high.
3. Dutch girl also marked Occupied Japan. 3¼" high.

BOTTOM ROW—
1. One of a group of half-bust bells made in Japan and imported from there in 1920's 1930's. If the idea was to illustrate American personages, this could represent Pochantas. 5" high.
2. Rather unusual figurine with sharp facial features. Marked as made in Czechoslavakia. Ceramic ball clapper. 5" high.

Figural Porcelains

TOP ROW—
1. Birthday Girl for June shown carrying traditional bridal attendant bouquet. 3¼" high.
2. Birthday Girl for July in form of a patriotic angel with Independence Day adornment. 3½" high.
3. Birthday Girl for August with suitcases suggesting a summer vacation. All Birthday Girls were made in Japan. 4" high.

MIDDLE ROW—
1. Half-figure resembling a children's Nanny. Marked "Made in Japan" with a clock trademark. 4¼" high.
2. The first annual Christmas ornament issued by Goebel Hummel Company of West Germany. Has the "V and bee" trademark. 1976, white bisque.
3. Ordinary figurine but with ceramic legs clapper. They are attached in the usual Japanese manner with a wire through two holes at back. Marked as made in Japan. 3" high.

BOTTOM ROW—
1. Half-figure resembling the nursery rhyme character, Wee Willie Winkie. Marked as made in Japan. 4¼" high.
2. Half-figure who may have been a housemaid. Japan. 4" high.
3. Another half-figure, this one probably a baker. Japan, 4" high.

Old and Fragile

TOP ROW—

1. Rare cowbell-shaped Crown Derby porcelain bell. Decoration is one of their so-called Japan patterns, always popular. Mark of Royal Crown Derby, England. Circa 1899.
2. Old glass jungfrauenbecher (also known as wedding or marriage cup bells) without swivel cup. One contention is that this type was designed in this manner so that the wine was drained from the upturned skirt in one drinking attempt. Inscription: "Alles gluck dem brautpaare" or "All happiness to him who drinks." German. 11" high overall.

MIDDLE ROW—

1. Meissen "Blue Onion" bell. The factory at Meissen, Germany, first of European porcelain makers, was established in 1710 with the origin of the famous crossed swords mark soon thereafter. Demands for Oriental patterns led to the development of the classic "Blue Onion" pattern about 1732. It was to typify the Japanese pomegranates, peaches and asters so it is only public opinion which sees onions in the design. This bell is an ageless product since the company, sold to Soviet Union in 1947 and now behind the Iron Curtain, is still producing. Since the latter part of the 19th century it has carried two crossed swords marks, one inside the bell and the other within design on outside. The bells are all handpainted so that individual bells will differ. 4½" high.
2. Fine porcelain table bell with applied flowers. Not marked but certified as about 1865. Purchased in Australia. 4½" high.

BOTTOM ROW—

1. Bristol ruby glass bell with graceful, clear half-steeple handle. Wooden clapper for safety in ringing. As with schoolbells, the handle is about one-half of the total height. England, 19th century. 11" high x 5".
2. Advertising bell for "Schweppe Table Waters" as seen around the shoulder. Marked Doulton Lambeth, England which was founded there about 1858, and whose products are now known as Royal Doulton. The old company made very few bells and this is judged very early 20th century. Hard glaze on pottery, wooden ball clapper on wire. 4½" high.

Belling Our Animals

The earliest type animal bell used was the crotal or sleigh bell. Rather than a round ball as we know it today, it was a birdcage style with pebble rolling around inside. Most American sleigh bells came from East Hampton, Connecticut, commonly known as "Jingle Bell Town." This nickname was the result of a preponderance of sleigh bell factories there, the first one being Barton Bell Company followed by Bevin Brothers in 1832. Due to lessened demand, the latter company is the only one of many still in existence.

Sleigh bells enlivened the monotonous snow travel and decreased the likelihood of a collision with another noiseless conveyance. Straps of up to forty bells are known and those of graduated sizes most popular. Crotals are attached with rivets or by an even better method, shanks and cotter pins.

TOP ROW—

1. #12 Long Distance cow bell made by Bevin Brothers in the 1940's. Made in one piece without rivets. Old bells with labels are harder to find so more valuable. Ordinarily worn on wrought iron loop around neck of cow. The sound is resonant enough to be heard a great distance. 4½" high, 3" x 4" base.
2. Goat bell, small with shrill tone. This one was for Nanny, with Billy getting one somewhat larger and deeper-toned as his neck bell. Purchased 1919 in Chamonix, France which is located in a section of the French Alps where goat milk and butter were used exclusively. These bells hung on the neck collar so the animals could be located.
3. #7 Holstein bell made by Blum Manufacturing Company of Collinsville, Illinois. Could be used for calf or sheep. Made of stamped sheet metal, folded and riveted on sides. Ball clapper. 3" high.
4. Small donkey bell from Greece. Modern but of the type seen in use on the islands. Brass. 2¼" high.
5. #1 deer bell from mountains of Spain. Has picture of deer on side with "CIERVO," Spanish word for deer, below. Well made and heavy, shows wear. Cast brass. 3¼" high. Horseshoe nail clapper.

MIDDLE ROW—

1. "Navajo" cow bell (brand name). Made by Bevin Brothers of New England. Copper plated steel with iron, cross-tongue clapper. 3¾" high x 4".
2. Typical of signal bell used on early Conestoga wagons. Used in later years on other conveyances. Bell 2½" high.
3. Two "Swedish" sleigh bells on original leather, so-called because they were popular on the Scandinavian Peninsula in mid-1800's. Made by Bevin Brothers. Triple-throated which means three slits across top, two extending to rim of bell and one stopping higher up. One bell is slightly larger to make a tuned pair. Brass.

BOTTOM ROW—

1. Pair of gazelle bells from Arabia. This small antelope is noted for softness of expression in his eyes as well as for grace and gentleness. Found in North Africa and Arabia.
2. Oxen bell from Portugal. Small but one of a string or could join others on collar. Made of sheet metal, folded and welded. 1" high.
3. Saddle chimes, an ornament for the saddle. Triple clappers for melodious sound. Of foreign make because of metric threads. Nickel plated over steel. Bell unit 9½" high.
4. Swinger. Originating in England, these small brass bells added pomp and gaiety to special events as they were mounted on the saddle or between ears of the horse. Called either "swingers" or "fliers." Bell unit 4½" high.

Belling our Animals

The old saying "I'll be there with bells on" originated with the drivers of the conestoga wagons as they faced the hardships and perils of journeys through dangerous territory. If he was forced to ask for help from another driver, according to custom, he was to give his bells to the rescuer. Therefore, it was a point of pride to overcome all handicaps and reach his goal with bells intact.

TOP ROW—
1. A pair of acorn-shaped falcon bells of the size used with the goshawk. This bird hunts from the fist so that when the quarry is flushed, it can easily overtake the rabbit, pheasant, or duck. Should she make a kill afar off in tall grass, the bells help in locating her. This pair is contemporary and made by the only known American maker, Peter Asborno.
2. Acorn-shaped sleigh bells, one of the most desired of many crotal variations. Ezra G. Cone patented this style and they were produced by Gong Manufacturing Company, East Hampton, Connecticut soon after their establishment in 1866. (Private collection).

MIDDLE ROW—
1. The most commonly known camel bells are the strings of cupped chimes and the claw-type but pictures show other styles were also used. This open type with elongated iron clapper comes from Egypt. Shows usage.
2. Small closed crotal turkey bell, not as loud as the open type. On worn leather neck strap. Tin.
3. Purchased in Formosa where hawkers were selling them as dog bells. Resembles the "evil eye" superstitious Chinese bells which were supposed to repel worldly evils.
4. Basenji dog bell. The Basenji is the oldest known breed of dog. Evidence of their use by Pharoahs five thousand years ago is shown on ancient Egyptian murals. Very intelligent breed but legend tells us they lost their bark so they would not be eaten by hungry leopards. This makes them poor watchdogs but still excellent hunters. This native hand-carved bell around their neck helps keep them located. Clapper is of wood but can be of bone. The breed was brought to the United States from Africa in 1941.

BOTTOM ROW—
1. Shaft bells. The solid brass housing arranges these bells so they would be fastened atop the shafts. The usual alignment places the large bell in center flanked by smaller ones at sides. Triple clappers in each gives melodious sounds as unit is moved. Probably made by a village harness maker which adds to their charm. Unit 12" high.
2. Turkey bell with strap broken from usage. Not only did the bell serve to scare off hungry hawks and animals but it enabled owners to locate the roaming flocks and find the nests of eggs. Open type with double clapper. Brass.

Belling Our Animals

Cow bells date back to the days of the ancient Romans when such were used on necks of sheep, goats, cows, and war horses. The first recorded casting was in Ireland. American pioneers left such work to the village blacksmiths who produced both cast and sheet metal types. These were attached to the lead cow in each herd to keep track of the grazing animals.

Camel bells hold a peculiar place in history as we read of entire caravans being found in dust storms because passing caravans heard their bells. These sounds also served to clear the streets of crowded villages so the burdened animals could pass.

TOP ROW—
1. Donkey bell discovered on neck of a donkey in Arabia then purchased from owner. Bold markings of SURAT may place its origin in India. Crotal shape, brass with unusual floral design.
2. Neck strap of free-swinging, double-throated bells on the original leather. The attachment is unique in that wire loops extend through holes in the top layer of the strap to expand between the leather layers and thereby hold the bells in place. Brass (Private Collection)
3. Typical water buffalo bell from Hawaii made of monkey-pod wood with Kanila wood clappers. Native warrior kings supposedly used the Kanila wood for carving their spears.

MIDDLE ROW—
1. Authentic Montagnard bamboo cowbell, handcarved by natives of Viet Nam. Visitor could not buy these in stores so had this one made. Outside clappers give soft clatter as the herd moves. These were seen in constant use.
2. Water buffalo bell from Java. Handmade with crude, elongated clapper. Brass. 3" high.
3. Riveted calf bell on original leather neck strap which is also riveted. Bell is made of stamped sheet metal with ball clapper. 3" high.

BOTTOM ROW—
1. Pair of crotal sleigh bells on old leather cut from strap of riveted bells. Has patent dates around under-side of each bell, "Pat. Oct. 24, '76 and May 14, '78." Shows double throating or two cross-cut slits. Brass.
2. Basque sheep bell. The Basque are professional sheepherders in the Pyrenees Mountains between Spain and France. Making these bells of rolled sheet copper, they are confident that no others could keep coyotes from feasting on their lambs. Sheep-bone clappers within the bulged metal give a cave-like echo that can be heard many miles away. Migratory herders have brought their bell-making techniques to the western part of the United States. 4½" high.
3. String of camel chimes taken from camel's neck in Dhahran, Arabia where such have been used since the days of Abraham. This is an average size camel bell with two progressively smaller bells as clappers. The string could be as long as eight or more. The claim is made that the tempermental camels are more contented with their chimes on. This set has linear markings to form design on each of the three bells. Brass. Largest bell 6" long.
4. Cow bell from Greece. Hand made of sheet copper with typical bulbous shape. The narrow nail-like clapper always hangs below the bell. Most such bells are rather small with resonant sound. 1¾" high.

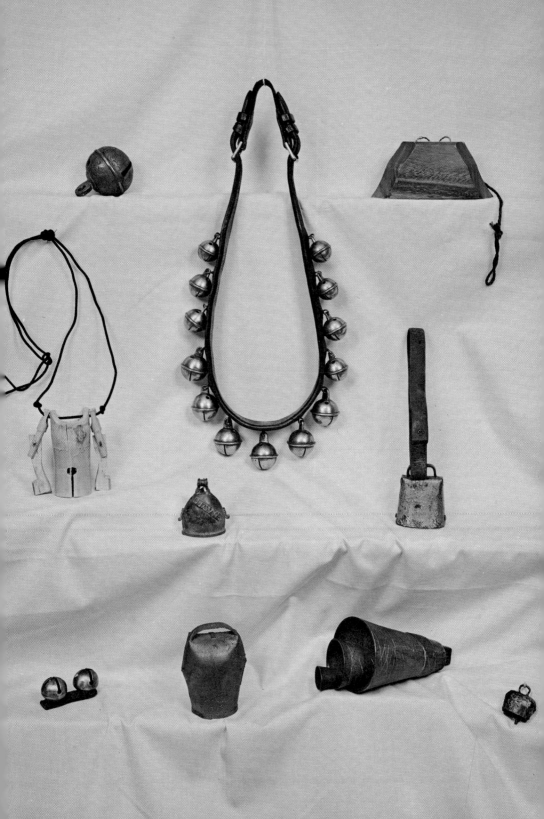

American Folk Art

1. Handmade by American Indians, these bells with symbols of nature, such as rain and sunrays, emphasize the Indians' dependence on good crops. Copper with copper clapper. 3" high.
2. Another American Indian product, heavily engraved with their symbols including thunderbirds which signify happiness. Pewter-like metal, wooden handle. Poor tone. 3½" high.
3. Underground kiln bell from Oxaca, Mexico but differing from the usual plain gun-metal gray. These clothes have been painted leaving the impression it is a girl of the black race. 3¾" high.
4. Festival bell from Oxaca, Mexico showing the many two-faced masks used in the celebrations. Made of their local clay and baked underground. 5" high.

MIDDLE ROW—

1. Teepee-shaped bell sold as Bicentennial souvenir by Amador, California Chamber of Commerce. It is crafted of white clay with madrona twig clapper hung by tanned rawhide deerskin. These are all native products of Amador County. Known as a bark house, the shapely bell has a "hidden gold" glaze to symbolize Mother Lode's rich earth. Limited edition. 5" high.
2. Ivory bell with whaleen bottom rim and clapper of bone. Native carving by Eskimo, Charles Shwooko. Purchased in Nome, Alaska. 5" high.
3. Ceramic wind bell in form of owl with miniature owl clapper. One-of-a-kind, made especially for the author. 6" high.

BOTTOM ROW—

1. Navajo Indian squaw. Made of clay. Modern. 4¾" high.
2. Pottery hippopotamus, creation of Todd J. Warner, a ceramic sculptor from Michigan. His intense interest in living things has ruled his life since childhood. Thus, following the idea that a little light whimsey can brighten our days, he develops this and many other such animal bells and figures. His works of art are exhibited across the country. 4¾" high.

Literary and Historical

TOP ROW—
1. Handle is Miguel de Cervantes, Spanish subject who wrote the first modern novel and one of the greatest, DON QUIXOTE. Born in 1547, a lifetime of hardships and bad luck was the background for the posthumous success of Cervantes' writings. His humorous approach to reality was the basis for DON QUIXOTE. Pictures around base of the bell are scenes from the story showing the country squire and his servant, Sancho Panza, as they set forth on their adventurous journeys. Gilded in the style of Spanish bells. Extra heavy, weighing 3¾ lbs. 8½" high.
2. Of the nine daughters of Zeus, supreme Greek god, who are known as the Muses, this handle is most like Urania. She is the Muse of Astronomy and has symbol of a globe and stylus. During the first years of their life, they were all alike then became individualized. "He is happy whom the Muses love" is expressive of their spirit of freedom from care. The body of the bell shows other Greek detail such as the lion medallions and egg-dart decor, both seen in the historical Parthenon. Bronze, (Private Collection) 6½" high x 2¾" dia.

   The next two bells are of the mysterious, but coveted group of bells known as Hemonys. The Hemony brothers were famous bell makers of the 17th century. Since their life spans do not coincide with the several bell inscriptions, researchers have concluded that spurious casters of later eras made use of the famous names with incorrect dating. Examples of Hemony bells are found with various handles, embossings, and inscriptions. The two shown here are inscribed "F. Hemony Me Fecit Anno 1569" meaning "F. Hemony made me in the year 1569."
3. A loop handle instead of the usual figure is rare. Embossing on front side shows the gargoyle or mythological bird sometimes found as figural handle but seldom as decoration. Has open beak with protuding tongue, raised wings, and is pinpricked. Back side shows medallion with rampant lion and a human figure. Seams show at sides. Brass. 4½" high.

BOTTOM ROW—
1. Hemony bell with handle representing a young warrior thought to be of the Children's Crusade of 1212. This was made up of thousands of children from France and Germany who set out to recover the Holy Sepulcher from the Moslems. This boy is seen in a helmet and chain mail vest, holding a club and shield with a strapped quiver resting near left foot. Embossing on base is typical with crusader scenes of men in combat and in prison. Bell is made in two parts so that handle screws into base, typical of 14th century bells. No seams are evident. 6½" high.
2. The Columbian Liberty Bell was the first deliberately created liberty bell. At the request of the Daughters of the American Revolution, the seven foot tall, thirteen thousand pound (one for each of the Colonies) bell was created for use at the 1893 Columbian Exposition in Chicago. Made of liberty-connected metals given by twenty-two thousand people over the world, it contained such items as a spoon of John Calhoun's, Abraham Lincoln's watch chain, and other famous relics. The Columbian bell served its purpose on the fairgrounds, but as the DAR planned to take it on a post-tour to promote world peace, it disappeared. No trace has been found despite the size of the elusive gem. As a Bicentennial Limited Edition, the McShane Bell Foundry descendants have issued the bell as pictured. Mounted with yoke and wheel, like large turret bells, it is suitably engraved and numbered #44. Fine tone, bell metal. Weighs 3½ lbs. 6 1/8" high x 5 1/4" x 6".
3. School bell carrying its full share of American history. In addition to the usual recess tidings, it saw Colonial use in warning of Indian attacks plus endless family use in announcing mealtimes to men in the fields. Marked "SWISS BELL—Trade Mark T.M. Co." Of bell metal with fine tone. 12" high with the customary proportion of handle being one-half of the overall height.

Literary and Historical

TOP ROW—

1. Lady with keys. Attire of fichu (neckerchief crossed at bosom) and apron plus keys in hand is suggestive of a housekeeper of the late 1700's. Simple camlet over the hair braids gives credence to a Lowlands origin. Brass. 3¼" high.
2. Maria Theresa (1717-1780), the member of the House of Hapsburg who became Queen of Hungary and Bohemia as well as Archduchess of Austria. A capable ruler and the mother of sixteen children among whom was Marie Antoinette. This daughter became Queen of France and died on the guillotine during the French Revolution. Made by Gerald Ballantyne and dated 1973. Fine bronze. 6" high.
3. Court jester, ready to cut a lively caper as he entertains his royal masters of the Medieval era. The traditional bells on his costume assist in claiming attention for his antics. Marked "England," early 20th century. Brass, 4" high.

MIDDLE ROW—

1. Hans Brinker, Dutch boy hero of the book, SILVER SKATES by Mary Dodge. Sacrificing his chance to win a skating race, Hans was responsible for the rehabilitation of his father. Has Dutch scenes around base of the bell. Of silicon bronze and made by the "lost wax process." A Gerald Ballantyne limited edition dated 1974. 6" high.
2. Eighteenth century English lady wearing farthingale with high collar, puffed sleeves and fan. Modified puffed-out hair style. Brass. 4" high.
3. French lady of the late 1700's. The mob cap shows this to be an at-home attire despite the stylish dress and fan. The custom of the times was for women to keep their heads covered at all times, even in their own abode. Brass. 4¼" high.
4. Henry David Thoreau, American naturalist and author of the 19th century, who gave up the niceties of civilization to live in a one-room cabin he built by Walden Pond. His journal, published as "Walden," told of many studies of nature as shown on the body of this bell. Bronze with fine tone. By Gerald Ballantyne, dated 1975. 6" high.

BOTTOM ROW—

1. Jenny Lind. Another pose for the famous Swedish nightingale (1820-1887) showing the flowered pannier skirt as she holds it up at either side. Bell is rounded on the bottom to conform to the side uplifts of the skirt. Brass. 4" high.
2. Mary, Queen of Scots, the 16th century personage doomed to tragedy but trusting to the end. This bell shows the farthingale front and back panels embroidered with thistles, emblematic of her country. The pose is developed from a 1578 portrait painted while she was imprisoned at Fotheringay Castle. Purchased in New Zealand with certification as made in mid-1800's. Probably an English product, of very heavy brass. Weighs 3 lbs. 7" high.
3. Sairy Gamp, the talkative, imbibing nurse in MARTIN CHUZZLEWIT by Charles Dickens. This is a story of his American travels. The old nursing slogan, "Don't be a Sairy Gamp, be a Florence Nightingale", evolved from this tale. Fine old brass. 4¼" high.

Crystal-Clear, Mostly New

Glass bells are difficult to analyze for several reasons. Not only was it a common practice among glass cutters to interchange designs, but the very shape of the article made signing difficult. Blanks made by one company then sent to others for decoration was a normal procedure. Modern tricks of turning broken goblets into bells only add to the confusion. Ways to determine whether an item was an original bell include checking for uneven grinding where the foot might have been broken off as well as studying the design for adaptation to bell or goblet — that is, whether or not it is upside down.

TOP ROW—
1. Lisemore pattern by Waterford of Ireland. This renowned company produced a high quality hand cut flint glass ware from 1729 to 1851. With lessening demand, it closed down to reopen in 1952. Modern. 4½" high.
2. Celeste pattern by Seneca Glass Company of Morgantown, West Virginia. In operation since 1892, this company is famous for blown glassware in Lead Crystal and colors. Modern. 4½" high.
3. By Cataract Sharp Company of Buffalo, New York, this example of their usual leaf motif with florals shows polished engraving. The company flourished from 1934 to 1948 and purchased custom blanks from other makers. This small wine glass with two-mold stem and blown bowl has a high degree of metal in the glass evidenced by its resonance. 4¾" high.
4. Hobstars, fans, swirled notched fluting, or pillars, make up the main design of this "Brilliant Period" (1895-1915) cut glass bell. Notched prism handle. Metal ball clapper on chain. 5" high.

MIDDLE ROW—
1. Alana pattern by Waterford Glass Company. Has all-over diamond-shaped cutting. All bells are signed by the company in form of a stamped name. Modern. 5" high.
2. Lead crystal bell from West Germany. All-over facet cutting around upper part of bell with more facets at top of the handle. Floral engraving in the blue band around lower part. Modern. 5" high.
3. A Cambridge-type bell with acid etching. Intended as such because of the position of the rose within the medallion. Cambridge of Ohio (1901-1954) was one of the few glass companies of that era who produced bells to match stem and tableware. 6" high.
4. Lace Point pattern by Seneca Glass Company. All bells from this company have unique clapper attachments in that the chain extends through the handle, fastened at the top. All have the Seneca script signature. Modern. 5½" high.

BOTTOM ROW—
1. To help promote the American Bicentennial, Waterford Glass Company produced this hand cut bell with "200" on front in copper wheel engraving. Only five men on their production line are qualified to do this intensive work. The bell sits in a heavy saucer base and is completely man-made. Ireland. 5" overall.
2. Made to commemorate the 100th anniversary of the birth of Winston Churchill by Edinburgh Crystal Glass Company in 1974. Numbered 63 of a Limited Edition of five hundred. Designed by David Hammond, Des., R.C.A. Scotland. 7½" high.
3. Delicate crystal bell with high degree of lead for resonance. Copper wheel engraving gives a pattern similar to Cambridge's Lily of the Valley. Arrangement of design gives credence to its bell origin but handle and shape seem otherwise. 5½" high.

Organizational and Fraternal

TOP ROW—
1. American Bell Association convention bell from Detroit, 1974. Commemorates the Motor City of the World's most famous automobile, the Model T Ford, a picture of which is found on the handle. Heavy, sand cast metal. 3½" high.
2. Official bell of the 1976 American Bell Association convention in Washington, D.C. Depicts the dome of the United States Capitol building with Goddess of Freedom atop. The original figure was designed by Thomas Crawford, American sculptor. The statue is 19½ feet high, weighs 7½ tons and cost nearly twenty-four thousand dollars. Erection was completed December 2, 1863. The figure holds a wreath and shield, has a sheathed sword and Indian headdress, symbolic of the part this group contributed to our heritage. Her position on the globe gives the idea of her protection of the American world. "E Pluribus Unum" is the wording on the band which encircles the globe. This convention bell was made by Valleau Foundry in Saugatuck, Michigan. Bronze. 5" high.
3. Souvenir bell with Kiwanis International emblem as handle. This world-wide men's service club has the motto, "We Build." Organized in 1915. Brass. 3" high.

MIDDLE ROW—
1. China bell with emblem of the Order of the Eastern Star, a fraternal order of Masons and close female relatives with present structure dating back to 1868. 2½" high.
2. District Deputy B.P.O.E. badge from 91st Annual Grand Lodge session Philadelphia, 1955. This national organization, Benevolent and Protective Order of the Elks, was organized in New York, 1868.
3. Souvenir B.P.O.E. bell with personal inscription to a member of the order in Paris, Illinois, 1900.
4. New York City American Bell Association convention bell for 1971. Made and donated by students of the public schools. Ceramic. 6½" high.

BOTTOM ROW—
1. A souvenir bell belonging to a deceased charter member of the Fort Scott, Kansas Rotary Club. Rotary is an international businessman's organization started in 1905 with motto of "unselfish service." Rotary emblem on bell with notation "Dairy Center of the Southwest."
2. Souvenir of Rainbow, an assembly of girls sponsored by the Order of the Eastern Star. Their purpose is to make the journey of life more worthwhile by setting early priorities and worthy goals. Ceramic. 3½" high.
3. 1975 American Bell Association convention bell from Monterey, California. Has Asilomar on the front which was the California state park on Monterey Peninsula, site of the meeting. The cypress tree dominates this coastal area as it fights the tides to cling to the crevices between the huge rocks. The forest is made up of twisted, gnarled skeleton-like trees, many two or three hundred years old. This is typified on the handle of the bell. Heavy bronze. 5½" high.

Religious Representatives

TOP ROW—
1. One of the copies of the renowned Saint Peter's bell atop the Basilica in Rome. Others may have a cross or other handle but this one has the Pope's triple crown, symbolic of his claim to temporal, spiritual, and purgatorial authority. Below this we see four cherubs, kneeling with hands on heads of serpents. This represents the triumph of church over sin. The twelve Apostles stand around the body of the bell in groups of three holding emblems of their office. These are Jude (ship), Peter (crossed keys), Andrew (cross), James the Greater (scallop shell), John (Chalice), Philip (cross and two loaves bread), James the Lesser (saw), Matthew (three purses), Thomas (carpenter's square and spear), Bartholomew (three flaying knives), Simon the zealot (open book and fish), Matthias (open Bible and axe). The overhanging cathedral lamps show spiritual light. When bell is lifted from the saucer, the fallen dove is seen in dimensional form. Such saucers have, at times, been used under religious bells although not so much during modern eras. These replicas were known to have been made before 1883 and again in the Holy Year 1950. 6" high overall.

MIDDLE ROW—
1. Our Lady of Farima handle bell, symbolic of a vision seen by three illiterate peasant children in 1917 at Fatima, Portugal. As they were tending their sheep, the lady in white, calling herself the Lady of the Rosary, appeared in a cloud. In return for their promise to offer their lives to God in atonement for worldly sin, she brings an end to World War I. However, she warns of further such wars unless transgressions cease and the worship of God triumphs. Scenes on upper body of bell are people in prayerful attitudes and sheep. Lower part of bell shows the shrine in Fatima, second in importance to Catholics. Of heavy brass, made in two parts, gilded. Spain. 6" high.
2. Miniature church bell from Fort Scott, Kansas Congregational Church as it was melted down for fund-raising purposes. Fire, a frontier hazard, often struck churches so these tiny replicas were shipped back East where affluency reigned. Specimens are now scarce in the Midwest. Tab on this bell says "Cong'l Ch., Ft. Scott, Kansas-Mem'l Bell, March 14, 1872." 5/8" high.
3. Sanctus bell used in religious rites. The three bells are suspended from a triangular frame representing the Trinity—Father, Son, and the Holy Ghost. Handle is shaped to represent the Sacred Heart. Original metric threading on the screws indicate a European make. From an old set of altar items.

BOTTOM ROW—
1. Bells used in Jewish religious rites are mainly decorative rather than having pious significance. This spice box is an important part of the orthodox Saturday evening Sabbath ritual when the aroma from the spices placed inside the small door is inhaled by the family. The blessings give hope that the remembrance of these odors will stay in their hearts during the oncoming week. Spice boxes are quite ornate due to Baroque period influence. Of delicate silver quilling, each removable piece is hallmarked. This includes bells, flags, and base. The mark shows maker's initials "HA," lion passant for sterling silver in England, leopard's head without crown for city of London, and letter K for year 1905-6. 9½" high.
2. Bevin altar chime with four varied-sized bells tuned to C chord. Each bell has triple clappers to give melodious sound. Small birds of St. Francis of Assisi perch on the four tree-like branches. The group of four represent the gospels; Matthew, Mark, Luke, and John with appropriate harmony among them. These are used in Greek Orthodox, Roman Catholic, and Episcopal churches at the Elevation of the Host or other important parts of the religious ceremony. Due to changing of liturgies, fewer of these chimes are being made. Modern. 5" high.

Oriental Chimes

1. Unusual type of crane gong. Made of lightweight brass and painted to emphasize details on bird. Due to its fabulous longevity, the crane stands for good fortune and extended life. India. 7" high.
2. Reproduction of an ancient carp gong that formerly hung in a Korean temple. The carp is the national emblem of Korea. Iron, from Japan. 6" long.

SECOND ROW—
1. Many nations, from Africa to the Orient, still revere the protective charm of blue beads. This Afghanistan necklace could have been worn daily to ward off evil spirits, not knowing when or how they could strike. Made of Indian silver.
2. Handle of this Javanese temple is their Goddess of Fortune sitting on two dragons. This same figure is found engraved on Javanese choice silver and embroidered on their fine linens. The base of the bell is in the shape of a Borobudur temple, a few miles from Jogjakarta. Men standing are guards for the temple, while the idea of dragons is to protect the deity. The Borobudur temples have hundreds of bells so decorated. Bronze, very heavy. Weighs 8 lbs. 12" high.
3. Handle is one of the poses of Hotei, deity of good fortune. Taoism embraces seven such gods and Hotei was the fat monk originally from China. He is always pictured as cheerful and fat, lover of children, and sometimes carrying a bag. This holds treasures for those who never worry about their troubles. The bell is Peking enamel on copper-plated, silver base. Panels on the hexagon bell show three flowers: peony for spring (love and affection), lotus for summer (fruitfulness), and chrysanthemum for autumn (joviality). Peking glass bead clapper. Marked CHINA. 5" high.

THIRD ROW—
1. Swayambunath temple bell so-called because the handle is fashioned after this important holy temple located in Nepal. Built 2,500 years ago by King Mana Deva, the shrine has the "eyes of God" gazing in every direction, keeping eternal watch over the people. This temple is also holy to the Hindus and is used for their religious rites which makes it one of the few temples in the world used by both Buddhists and Hindus. 5½" high x 2¼" diameter.
2. Dancer's bell used by young girls of India as they perform temple rites as part of worship. Can be used singly or with others in necklace, anklet, or ornament for finger or toe. Modern from India. (Private collection.)
3. Pelican handle bell. Since their homeland is surrounded by water, it is only natural for Japanese art works to show many such waterfowl. The Melanesians originated the myth telling that at one time all pelicans were black. To disguise himself, one started covering his exterior with pipe clay. During the process another pelican came by, wondered what unusual creature that was, then struck him dead. Since that time, all pelicans have been a mixture of black and white. Brass, made in china. 3¼" high.
4. Shaman Fortune Bells. A Shaman is a medical man who cures sickness, has charge of the communal sacrifices and escorts the souls of the dead to the Other World. This is part of a religious phenomena, Shamanism, found in Asia, Siberia, Ural Mountains, and some North American tribes. Labeled "Oriental Fortune Bells, this rattle is shaken by the Shaman. Has seen usage. 10" long.

BOTTOM ROW—
1. Peony flowers on base of this enamelled bell signify signs of spring and omen of good fortune. Conch shells on the handle and base below handle represent Buddha's voice. Peking glass clapper. Marked CHINA. 4¾" high.
2. Anklet arrangement whose edge is many tiny bells. Traditionally worn by Hindu women of high caste. The same type anklet bell is seen in pictures of Siva, Lord of Dance. This old specimen shows signs of wearing through of the metal on back side of bells. Private collection.
3. Handle is Ho Hsien-Ku, one of the eight Immortals of Taoism. As Patron of the House, she walked the countryside seeking bamboo sprouts for her sick mother even though her own immortality diet consisted only of powdered mother-of-pearl. Her emblem is the lotus seen across her shoulders. Bell base shows large bat on either side for happiness. Marked CHINA. 4" high.

Sundry Silver Gems

TOP ROW—
1. A 1975 Mother's Day bell issued by Danbury Mint in Westport, Connecticut. This company is engaged in making and selling commemoratives and is not connected with governmental agencies. The handle is the classic American rose, representing the traditional gift of flowers for Mother. Sterling silver. 4" high.
2. Scene on handle is "Spirit of '76," famous painting of the Revolutionary War by A. Willard. Silverplated. Holland. 2½" high.

MIDDLE ROW—
1. Kewpie handle, one of the pixie-type figures created by Rose O'Neill who used them in LADIES HOME JOURNAL illustrations as early as 1909. Within a few years the demands of children brought forth the kewpie dolls plus a rash of novelties and trinkets. Present day kewpie collectors are numerous. Kewpie stands as handle with Rose O'Neill on back base of figure. Silverplated. 3" high.
2. Modern treatment of the old wedding cup bell. This one has traditional wedding rings represented by holes at top. Silverplated bell and ball clapper. 6¼" high.
3. El Camino Real bell showing the old bells placed in front of the 18th century missions. These were established along the King's Highway now known as U.S. 1. The southern part of this highway follows the approximate path of the missions between San Diego and a point near San Francisco. The light posts are replicas of these old bell standards. Holland. Silverplate. 3" high.

BOTTOM ROW—
1. Handle shows Paul Revere making his famed midnight horseback ride to arouse the Minutemen in 1775. His silversmithing activities of later years contributed many fine bells, mostly of the large variety. Holland. Silverplate. 2½" high.
2. Silver dragon bell. The Chinese dragon belies its terrifying appearance in that it is a mild, passive creature, symbolizing goodness and strength. It has the power to be visible or invisible as it so desires. In autumn it descends to the waters but rises to the skies in the spring, denoting the return of fertility to the earth. Dragon lore is one of the earliest of Chinese nature myths and only the emperors have been allowed to use three or five clawed dragons in their Coat of Arms insignia. Commoners were limited to the four clawed symbol. If they intruded on the privilege of the emperor, decapitation was possible. Besides three chief species of dragons, there is a particular type known as ku t'ung lung or "dragon of old bronzes." It has a slender body similar to a lizard with a curving, split, or cleft tail. Since its four feet were usually three clawed, the dragon on this bell seems to fit the description. Silver. 3½" x 2¾" diameter. (Private Collection.)

Taps and Twirlers

TOP ROW—
1. Damascene or Toledoware windup bell from Toledo, Spain in form of snail which rings by pushing neck. Design is a double eagle with small crown above. Recalling the brief Austrian Hapsbug rule of Spain, the designers selected their crest for decoration. The two headed eagle was also used by the Russian czars of the Romanov dynasty. Other inlaid gold designs are florals, leaves, and birds. Damascening, the hammering of gold or silver wires into the black base metal, dates from the Roman Empire. Swords of the Far East were then done in this style but as civilization spread westward, so did the appeal of the art. Toledo swords were so noted for their excellence that Spain has taken over most of the industry. Modern. 6¼" x 2½".
2. Rare tap bell with gilt ormolu leaves, flowers, and grape clusters over brass bell. The four turquoise stones give color. On marble base, which makes it resemble the slave bells used on French boudoir tables during 19th century. France. 4" x 4½" diameter. (Private Collection.)

MIDDLE ROW—
1. Regular twist bell completely covered by gold filigree. Solid gilt bottom. Typical of French or Austrian artisians during the past century. 3" x 3½" diameter. (Private collection.)
2. Slave call bell used on milady's boudoir table to summon personal maid. Known to have many types of ornaments on top such as this bird, a mirror, candle holder, bird's nest and plain crescent. Mother-of-pearl mollusk shells rest on a filigree brass circle decorated with clusters of brass grapes. Marble base. French. 19th century. 6" high.
3. Brass tap bell with outside striker. This mechanism is atop a hand carved crouching gnome carrying fagot of wood on his back. Typical of German Black Forest wood-carvers but purchased in France. 7" high. (Private collection.)

BOTTOM ROW—
1. Rampant, or rearing, lion which is representative of objects made in the city of London. Bell is of the twist type. 8¾" high. (Private collection.)
2. Tap bell with filigree decoration around unusual striker handle. Below is silk embroidery on satin, padding the shelf which was used as place to lay calling card after announcing presence. Such card receivers were popular last half of 19th century. Purchased in France. 5½" high. (Private collection.)
3. Silver twist bell. Shows boy paddling canoe among cattails with detail on back as well executed as that on front. Marked K & S on bottom, mark used by Kirk & Smith, Baltimore, Maryland 1815-1818. Samuel Kirk, partner in this company, later (1828) introduced Kirk Repousse, the flower and foliage design, sometimes called "Baltimore Silver." 7½" high. (Private collection.)

Sarna's India

TOP ROW—

1. Plain sweetmeat bell. Many rich Indian goodies are sold in shops where the makers sit in center of their displays to wrap each purchase in a green palm leaf. If a choice is far from his reach, the shopkeeper maintains his balance by holding onto a bell hanging from the ceiling. When business is brisk, sweetmeat bells are prevalent over the city. 2" high.
2. Enamelled elephant's bell. Since the days of Mogul emperors, elephants have been decorated with bells. The birthdays of the Maharajas were celebrated by elephant parades with howdahs (special chair) atop the elephant for the honoree. 4" high.
3. Engraved bakra bell. A common sight in the large cities of India is the snake charmer who has a cobra in a basket swaying to the music of the man's flute. Also, there is often a bakra (goat) ladened with bells and monkey on his back. The monkey is asking for coins and bells call attention to the act as it progresses on its way. 2½" high x 2¾" diameter.
4. Engraved Bheestee bell. Used by water carriers as they fetch water from wells, springs, or streams for drinking or bathing. Some use goat skins to hold the liquid, others have buckets hanging from shoulder poles. Males are not welcome in the harems but Bheestees are allowed. He rings his bell to sell his water. 2½" high.
5. Enamelled Tanga bell. A Tanga is a one-horse carriage with two wheels. Curtains are pulled if ladies are passengers. These are a form of taxi and licensed locally. Bells on horse's necks warn pedestrians. 2¾" high.

MIDDLE ROW—

1. Engraved munshi bell. Sitting cross-legged under a canopy behind a small wooden desk sits a bespectacled man with bamboo pen over his ear. The munshi, or writer, is ready to reach for writing materials as illiterate customers stop for his services. Between customers he puffs on his water pipe and rings his bell to let people know he is available. A munshi is highly respected by the community and beloved by children who wonder at his great knowledge. 2½" high.
2. Enamelled cow bell. Hindus consider cows sacred and allow them to wander freely in the streets, fed by the people. The Queen cow wears a bell and her milk is not touched by common people. 3" high.
3. Enamelled beggar bell. Begging is a profession in India so that millions of people live on the coins they collect in outstretched hands. To attract attention, they show wounds or sit on spikes plus carrying rattles or bells. All worldly belongings are often carried across their shoulders on a bamboo pole. A bell is tied to this pole so it rings as they wander and collect alms. Triple clappers. 3" high.

BOTTOM ROW—

1. Wedding bell. The mysticism and beauty of the elaborate weddings in India are enhanced by the use of bells. They accompany the procession of the bridegroom, his parents and relatives, as they make their way through the streets to the home of the bride. The Pandit (priest) chants hymns and rings bells while reading Sanskrit and the honored couple is asked to participate by interim bell ringing during the two or three hour ceremony. 4½" high.
2. Plain temple bell. At daybreak the High Priest of the Hindu temples prepares the gods for worship by the people. As the worshippers come with offerings, they ring the bell hanging in front of their particular god so their prayers may be heard. 2½" high.
3. Engraved phool flower bell. City squares are filled with florists ringing bells and shouting names of their flowers. As the evening bustle reaches a peak, husbands buy strings to take home, young married couples buy them to sprinkle on beds, then toss in the river during morning bathing. 2¼" high.
4. Plain buffalo bell. Water buffaloes are considered sacred in Southern India and are worshipped along with cows as part of the Hindu religion. 3" high.

The term, "Bells of Sarna" does not refer to an area in India but to an unusual individual known as S. S. Sarna by bell lovers over the world. Born in Pakistan but receiving higher education degrees in the United States, he has been in the import business for several decades. Now a citizen of the United States, Mr. Sarna is an active member of the American Bell Association and an inspiration to all collectors. "Bells of Sarna" are handmade by Indian families who have passed their techniques down through generations.

Handle Happenings

TOP ROW—
1. Rooster handle is a fine example of Art Deco period during the 1920's and 1930's. The name for this era was derived from the Paris Exhibition in 1925 and emphasized simple, angular lines. The bell is of soft brass and rooster seems to be bronze which may make it an assembled, yet desirable, item. Purchased in Europe. 6¼" high.
2. Pixie handle on this old bronze bell with worn, brass finish. English folk tales identify pixies with the spirits of infants who have died before baptism. The Pixy-monarch holds his court like Titania and sends his subjects on their assigned duties. Marked "Rd. 7892" which, according to the London Patent Office, places it as designed prior to September, 1909. Reproductions now made. 3" high.

MIDDLE ROW—
1. A Bicentennial commemorative by Gerald Ballantyne with emblems around body of bell. The eagle is the official emblem of the United States symbolizing power, courage, freedom and immortality. The Great Seal of the United States is affixed to official documents, the Liberty Bell stands for American independence, and the "Spirit of '76" scene is a famous painting by A. Willard. The latter depicts Colonial troops fighting their way through the smoke and din of battle. Bell is of fine bronze with the usual "B" monogrammed clapper. 6" high.
2. Griffon handle showing the Roman and Greek mythological creature, half lion and half eagle, with wings extended as though in flight. The designs around body of bell show Florentine influence and the Romans were known to use the griffon as decoration in altar appointments, friezes, and hangings. Copy of a bell of Italian origin. 5" high.
3. Ecstatic Bacchante dancer (circa 186 B.C.), holding tambourine and traditional staff. Other symbols of these drunken orgies dedicated to Bacchus, Roman God of wine and the vintage, are in the design on side of bell. Included are more musical instruments, ivy tendrils, staffs, and wine ewers. These are centered by the Bacchante cameo with traditional hairstyle. 4½" high. (Private collection.)

BOTTOM ROW—
1. Helmeted knight representing medieval times. The replaced handle on this bell is of solid brass. Modern. 6" high.
2. Ram's head handle, perhaps symbolical of the Greek mythological good luck belief. Could represent the zodiacal constellation Aries. Floral engraving on bell worn due to high buffing. Brass. 4" high.
3. Giralda Tower handle, commemorative of the famous Seville, Spain cathedral. The tower was originally a Moslem minaret from which muzzeins called the faithful to prayer. When the Moors left Spain in 1492, the belfry was a Renaissance addition and is probably the only example of a Moslem minaret becoming a Christian belfry. Scenes around base of bell are La Pinta, La Nina, and Santa Maria, ships of Columbus as he headed for the New World. Seville, Spain is a sister city to Kansas City, Missouri and the Plaza shopping district has a replica of this Giralda Tower. Just before World War II, these and similar bells, often with an interchange of bases and handles, started being produced in Spain. All had a gilded exterior that may show signs of wear or attempts at removal. 6½" high.

Nodding Personages

Nodders are so-called because an attached weighted clapper within the body makes the head nod as it moves. These animated figures appeal to young and old. One special usage was in the tea houses of Old China. As the pilgrims stopped for refreshments, their movements started the motions of the figurines and provided amusement for the weary travellers. Other background has been given in previous books.

TOP ROW—
1. Early unmarked German lady nodder. Unusual pose with oversized basket. Fine detail, ceramic weight on stick. The flat metal balance-piece indicates an older nodder than those with round pins. 5" high.

MIDDLE ROW—
1. Catherine of Aragon nodder by Gerald Ballantyne, past president of the American Bell Association. Catherine of Aragon lived in the early 16th century, daughter of the Spanish king who started Columbus on his voyage to the New World. As the first wife of Henry VIII and mother of Mary I, she has a prominent place in English history. This nodder is so precisely balanced that the head nods over one thousand times. Fine bronze, numbered and signed. 4¾" high.
2. Street vendor in personage of a typical Scotsman with beard, sitting on a stool covered with fancy "throw." In his hand is a bottle of ointment with more in his apron pocket on which is written "Pommad" with price of item. The pomade seller uses the drum and bell at his feet as well as voice to attract customers. Excellent details show the Scotch plaid of outfit. Old and rare, heavy bronze. 4½" high.

BOTTOM ROW—
Oriental man and woman nodders, of delicate coloring indicative of early German porcelains. Fine detail showing individual fingers and nails, also the individual hairs on head and their teeth. Hands move on wires and the heads via metal-weighted clappers. Mark of 19th century Dresden porcelain factory on back of each figure. 7¼" high.

National Harmonies

TOP ROW—

1. "Hei Tiki" handle, of great significance to the New Zealand Maori people. Shaped in form of a human embryo in remembrance of the premature child born to a wife of one of their gods. She tied the half-formed child in her "tiki-tiki" or topknot of her hair and threw him into the sea. Found by the God of the Sea, he was nurtured to maturity, returned to his mother and became the progenitor of the Maori race. Solid clapper formed in shape of a human head. From New Zealand, 4¼" high.

2. An Around-the-World Shopper's Club gift of early 1950's. Attached tag explained the fishermen use this type of bell on Lake Como, Italy. Attached to a large lighted cork which supports fishing nets, this makes the lake into a huge, floating fairy village with bobbing lights and magic bell tinkles. Enamelled finish. Lightweight. 3½" high.

3. Viennese bronze bell with branch and leaves design. Well-made and heavy, though modern. Purchased in Austria. 4" high.

MIDDLE ROW—

1. Art Noveau bell in shape of flower with leaves and branch handle. Enamelling on the solid brass base gives look of stone. Circa 1890. Clapper missing. 4½" high.

2. Ornate gold repousse over chrome bell. Nailsea type glass handle. Unusual treatment for this small call bell. 4½" high x 2" diameter. (Private collection.)

3. Victorian call bell with ebony handle. Table bells have been made in England since reign of Elizabeth I. This latter 19th century style is typical of those made in Ireland at that time. 6½" high.

BOTTOM ROW—

1. Cameroon native with drinking horn, a prized possession. Early ones were of cow's horns and also glass. Records from as early as 400 A.D. mention the glass drinking horns, both clear and amber. Besides the necessary water, natives use the horns for drinking palm wine. Polished brass. Modern from Africa. 7" high.

2. Souvenir "bobby" or policeman's hat from England. Made of bronze-like metal. Metropolitan Police crest on front is centered with ER, abbreviation for Elizabeth Reign. Marked "Made in England, H. Seener, Ltd."

3. Stylized branch handle, black vertical lines on the cast bronze bell. Modern from Israel. 5" high.

Of This Era

TOP ROW—
1. Of fine china, this bell is marked Tokiro, Japan. Dates back to 1930's or 1940's. 3½" high.
2. Ruby glass bell with scenic band of poetical landscapes by Giorgione, Venetian painter of the late 15th century. Modern from Murano, Italy. 5¼" high.
3. Mini bell with matching lantern (not shown) is produced by Coalport, established in England 1750. The company became a part of the Wedgewood group in 1969. Trademark inside bell. Fine bone china. 1¾" high.
4. Small tea bell by Coalport. This is one of several English companies specializing in bone china, a glazed hard-paste clay with high degree of translucency. Marked as modern item. 4" high.

SECOND ROW—
1. Handblown replica of an English wedding bell made in two pieces with piece of styrofoam in hollow handle. This holds the metal ball chain clapper. Made by Pilgrim Glass Company, in production since 1608, in Ceredo, West Virginia. Modern. 7½" high.
2. Modern Imari made in Communist China. Since bells were not known in the old patterns, craftsman Ralph Walker has made this tea cup into a bell, complete with bead clapper and cherry wood handle. 5" high.

THIRD ROW—
1. A Bernardaud product made in Limoges, France, home of many fine porcelain factories. Unusual white bisque clapper in form of double ram's head. 3½" high.
2. Handblown crystal bell with latticino or milk white twists in handle. Made in Pairpoint glasshouse in Massachusetts where freeblown glass artisans are at work. This may be the last generation to master this art due to its demanding nature. The workers use no molds, only their innate sense of beauty and balance. There are few current apprentices The handpainted enamel flower design holds the Pairpoint signature "P." Limited Edition. 1¾" high x 5" diameter.
3. Just for fun—a Coca Cola glass bell made in Italy. Modern, design on three sides of bell. 5¼" high.

BOTTOM ROW—
1. Bone china bell by Hammersley, a subsidiary of Spode China Company. Typical shape of mid-20th century. Green Hammersley mark inside bell. From England. 5¾" high.
2. Hand painted Italian pottery bell with rooster, the alarm clock of rural areas. 5½" high x 4" diameter.

OF THIS ERA (cont.)

TOP ROW—
1. Delicate china bell with hand applied flowers. Has permanent Lefton China trademark inside which indicates it is their finest product. The complete mark includes company name, Lefton crown, the words "hand-made" and Reg. U.S. Pat. Off. Flowers have brilliants in centers. 2½" high.
2. Another Lefton hand painted bell with permanent trademark. 2½" high.
3. Fine china bell by Bareuther in Bavaria, West Germany. Bead-chain clapper. 6½" high.
4 and 5. Pair candlestick holders of translucent china. The floral design is signed by Bocacui with words "hand-painted" inside bell. 4¼" high.

SECOND ROW—
1. Owl tea bell of fine glazed china. Has actual beads for eyes. From West Germany. 4¼" high.
2. China bell with applied flowers. Paper label indicates "EW-Japan". 3" high.
3. Hand painted Italian pottery with bluebird, emblem of happiness. Signed Prof. Santarelli, Gualno, Italy. 4" high.
4. Typical mold for the hand painters of latter 19th century. Unsigned but done in manner of R. S. Prussian porcelain of which few bells are known. 3¼" high.

THIRD ROW—
1. Moss Rose bell. The beloved rose has found flavor with mankind since the days of the Crusaders. The Cabbage Rose was most fragrant in the garden of King Midas so this Moss Rose variation was to have the same qualities and is so-called because of the mossy projections seen on stems and around buds. Reaching the height of popularity in mid-1800's, the Moss Rose is still a favorite decoration. Modern. From Japan.
2. First annual Norman Rockwell bell dated 1975 showing a twenty-year old painting, "Young Love." The tender scene is full of springtime nostalgia. Produced by Gorham Company, this fine china bell has walnut handle and silverplated clapper. 9" high.
3. Another hand painted bell using the old mold. Actual time of painting hard to determine but signed by L. Propst. 3¼" high.
4. Same as one just described but signed by Dorothy Cawlfield and done in recent years.

BOTTOM ROW—
1 and 2. Late 19th century porcelain dinner sets often included a servant's call bell. This was discontinued for a time during mid-1900's but Aynsley Porcelain Company of England has revived the custom. These two bells match current sets, Pembroke and Famille Rose. Both have dainty wedding ring handles. 3½" high.

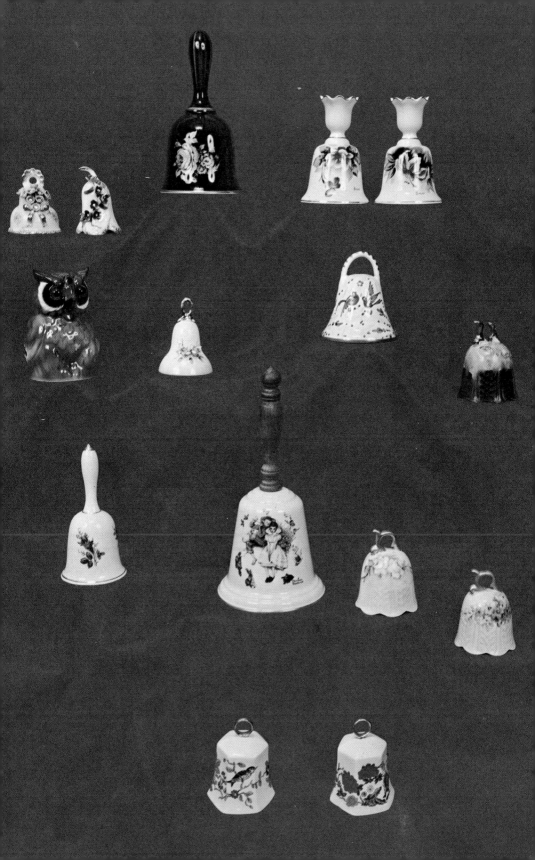